SCATTERED THOUGHTS: A STREAM OF CONSCIOUSNESS

**Poetry and Prose
by Felicia Guy-Lynch**

dedication

TO ALL THOSE STRIVING
TO MAINTAIN SALVATION

Contents

Just Thinking

Many denominations, supposed to be as one
Legalism makes no room for fun

Faith belief in unverified thought?
Question what you've been taught?

Difference between religion and spirituality?
Humans multiple in dimensionality?

Correction in subjective errors?
Muslims are peaceful. Babylon sends out them
terrors

"War on Terror"
More like, "War on Error"
Prepare as we usher into the New Age of the Wa-
ter Bearer

Solitude
Seldom seen, more admired
Seldom heard, more inspired

Fitting in concerns us when we get grown
From time to time, best to be alone

Tolerating other's foolishness keeps you a good
extrovert
Calling out your own foolishness makes you the
best introvert

Discern fakers
Make fun of users and takers

When you look in the mirror, like what's in sight
If you don't, you're scared, might take the near-
est flight

Accept you holistically
Par with those who do just as equally

Learn to be happy alone
We're responsible for our happiness, we set the
tone

Distance yourself, you'll know who cares
Rest could care less, preoccupied with their own
affairs

Stolen Innocence

She knew as a young girl
Fairy tales not of this world

Teeth she'd kiss
Wasn't asking for it. Didn't deserve this

Wasn't right
Too scared. Kept lips shut tight

Too embarrassed to let anyone know
Feeling alienated, deep down, dear not let it
show

Performed phallus pleasing deed
Male desires she'd feed

Went on for months on repeat
She was 8. Teen girls couldn't compete

Void of consent
Opposite sex grew to resent

Not her fault
Kept it secret like they do in the occult

Macho in her eyes. Coward in mine
If her hormones were raging, would it just be
fine?

Their selfish exploits gave a bad sensation
Got older. Found out it was molestation

Parents thought otherwise
Started to think they were full of it, only told lies

Lesson learned?
Self-respect is earned

Pa

We all miss you
The amount of pain endured, no clue, nothing
new

Left fatherless
Who could care less?

Reality check: life's not full of magic
Death was too tragic

Life hard to maintain and make
Easy to thoughtlessly take

Wish you survived those 9 bullets like 50 cent
Miss hugging and smelling your cologne, such a
beautiful scent

Wherever you are, rest in peace
Pain of you gone never seems to cease

Backstabbers
Too bitter
Like a night critter

Can't see them, make so much noise
Should be actors, fake with such poise

Less chances of getting them with less friends
Quite divisive, stifling dividends

Piss on your head, tell you it is rain
Envious, full of disdain

True colours never change
Spectrum of loyalty, lowest on the range

Powerful when back's turned
Mind who you eat with. Might get burned

Two-faced: which face to slap first?
Let me know as I end my last verse

Mercy

Birthed by my mother
Untimely death of my father

Gave my life to the Heavenly One
Gonna face God when this life is done

The walk got intense, pains harder to bear
Hell was a definite fear

Secured my place in heavenly bliss
Watch Him blow the Adversary with his mighty
fist

Struggled with spirituality
Caught up in religiosity

Peace of mind for a time no more
Bruises from fighting demons got real soar

Tears shed like a leaf
Attributed to distractions from denominational
beef

Physical rituals can't replace spiritual decay
Too many false prophets leading the people
astray

Take heed to the righteous ecclesiastic
Revelations reveal world more hectic

Future looking doomier
Without the light, spirit will grow gloomier

Melinated Wombman

Take pride in the kink in your hair
Like Black Panther's rocked afros, Black Power
they declare

Worry not about the high paying position
India Aries' "I Am Not My Hair" resonate with
your cognition

Black men used to want us
Other women more appealing. Don't seem to
cuss

Perpetuating jungle fever
Leave it to Beaver

Maintain your intrinsic self-worth
Commodifying your ASSets shouldn't have been
given birth

Hyper-sexualization of our identity needs to
stop
Cover up in those videos. Quit the booty pop

Forget B.E.T, "Black Enslavement Television"
Pride about the right things should meet timely
decision

Melinated Nubian King

Family more important than your gear
You sowed the seed. Your child she'll bear

More than just cookie-cutter videos
Manhood isn't just pretty hoes

Quality over quantity
Seek gems void of vanity

You used to want Black women
Must Willie Lynch deepen?

Deactivate that chip
Republicans and Democrats? More like Blood vs.
Crip

Value the mind not just the pussy
Easy way is destruction. Don't be a wussy

Love thyself. Misogyny obsolete
No real woman? Never be complete

Put down that gun. Make peace
Utilize your dome. Ignorance cease

Politricks

Prosperity Gospel
Got most under a spell

Sense over dollars
Not just poppin' collars

Rich call the shots. Roll the dice
Poor labor. Paying the price

Pulpit pimps exploit the poor
Motto is, 'more and more'

Electors for office
Came from caucus

Don't care who is in charge: human rank all the same
Boss for a time: transitory just like fame

Taxes sky rocketing
Can't blame thieves for stealing from the rich.
Keep pocketing

Wide gap between have and have nots
Cash rules everything around us. Chasing gwop like robots

Less conservatives and liberals
More revolutionaries. Fearless radicals

Good deeds don't feed the socially marginalized
Stealing from the rich should get legalized

Keep within still when outsides full of chaos
After punching out, make sure to be your own
boss

4 Letter Word

Has me in a rat race
On to the next comforts of a new face

Didn't last
Fell in too fast

Is it real or an illusion?
My broken heart brought me to this conclusion

Infatuation prolonged?
By my perception of this word, I've been
wronged

Played out ideal?
Lie tried to make real?

People change
Would be nice if mutual in exchange

With God, it's unconditional
Hurt people manipulate vulnerabilities.
Turn ammunitional

Pursued a soulmate
Believed, 'I love you,' fell for the bait

Gave away. Can't get back
Trust in guys I lack

Learned to first love me
Stop expecting it from him. Seeing what I want
to see

Utilize my wiz
Seeing things for what it really is

Be the lover others want to find
Might be so rare. One of your kind

Love Lessons

Love to let go of that person
Holding on might make that pain worsen

Longing for someone who doesn't love you is
like embracing a cactus
Tighter you squeeze, more it pains: oozing sore
pus

Don't hold onto someone who doesn't care to
lose you
Matters not what you say or do

Feelings shared. Can't undo
Let them go. Happy with or without you

To love and be loved validates the interconnec-
tivity for the human presence
Sharing is always caring. Enjoy life in it's very
essence

Keep affection genuine. Lasting resonance
Call out pretension. Trample on dissonance

People full of hate make an unrealistic demand
People full of love prompt feelings of giving.
Watch it expand

Love not freely given? Not worth receiving
Waste no time to lament and continue grieving

Commonality of boyfriend, girlfriend and friend
All have 'END' at the end

Love is a game. Enjoy the ride.
Think twice: is it really greener on the other
side?

Your good was the best
Created your mental unrest
Grass was burned
Regain respects once earned

First love rarely lasts a lifetime
Honeymoon stage ripest at its prime

Nice for how long it could last
Find another. Relive what you thought would
past

Issues between lovers
Worked out under covers

Relationship between boy and girl
No inputs from the whole wide world

Fall for someone who deserves your heart
Not for someone who plans to break it apart

Accepting your baggage. Helping you unpack
Can't handle their own? They're simply wack

Two I's make a team
Selfless it would seem

Treated like an option? Need to be dropped.
They don't care

Treated like a priority? Like a gem: they're very rare

Show your love. Give it true meaning
Lip service and empty deeds simply demeaning

Heart never too broken for repair
Being vulnerable. Would you dare?

New love comes in due season
Smiling for no reason

On your mind
All the time. One of a kind

Loved despite weakness
Held with high esteem through their meekness

Can't sleep. In love in totality
Dreams better than reality

No one's worth the chase
A person who appreciates you walks with you at a steady pace

Not everyone you love will love you back
Make sure to love yourself. True validation you won't lack

Hurting the one's that love us
Fight and fuss
Appreciate them while they are here

Regret not doing so. Knowing that they were
once near

Farewells with no signs? Very painful
Love with no limits? Oh so beautiful

Hard to climb out of. Requires you to fall
Keep from getting hurt. Building that wall

Love who is far and want to see you
Than those who are close and should have out-
grew

Wrong person doesn't deserve one's commit-
ment
Will create feelings of resentment

The break up. Two parted
Who dumped who? Doesn't matter. Love de-
parted

One thing for a fling to do
Another for someone to wake up to

Finding love will tire you mentally
Just be you. It will come. Naturally

Battle of Sexes

Raging hormones. High school
Got your freak on? Considered cool

Reality for the male
Far for the female

Not into feminism
I dislike chauvinism

Hypocrisy of patriarchy
Revive the matriarchy

Girl. Can You Relate?

Roman antics
Pretty boy. On to your tactics

Sounds too good to be true. Could be a fake
Don't wanna get hurt again. Yet missing 100% of
the shots I don't take

Better safe than sorry. Prevention is better than
cure
Half-full or half-empty? I'm not really sure

Maintain your rep. Keep composure
'Gezebelian' label. Humiliating exposure

Pregnancy pacts
Illicit acts

Babes having babes. Got them in a carriage
To hell with all that jazz about saving it for mar-
riage

Too excited to wait. All your friends did it
Waited any longer? Bad case of blue clit

Just like dudes. Bad case of blue balls
Wanting to bust a nut with girls they'd find in
malls

To keep from getting hurt? Protect emotionality
Hoping for endless ecstasy in minutes of sensu-
ality

Beautiful shaft. Protrude
Forget the predictable. Stare in the nude

Parents mad. Should have held on to serenity
Gave in. Dumping abstinence and chastity

Past furious
Probably did it. Cat was curious

Give away something. Can't get back
Would be worse in the back of his lac

First time. Can't cherish for life
So disastrous. Screw out of strife

Should have waited
Too elated

Feeling empty. Growing cold
Regrets of not doing what they were once told

Yearned passion
You were a trend like the game of fashion

Stuck in idealism
Rude awakening of realism

Fun lasted just as long as the play did
You are not at an auction. No need to bid

With someone for money to alleviate expenses?
Really foolish. Lost your senses

Mad it didn't last
Glad he's in the past

Sex. No longer the sweet escape
Not your fault. Blame this on the rape?

Yet to heal
A prey. Predators you appeal

Wallow not in self-pity
Take back your self-worth. That's the nitty gritty

Stop giving it up to get love
Lasts forever when it comes from above

If you lie with dogs, you will rise with flees
Remember this for the future please

Just Live

Be carefree. Keep from being careless
Don't try hard. Art of being effortless

Distrust between anyone creates a rift
Treat each other's presence as a gift

Love people. Use objects
Flip it? Become social rejects

Justify no resentment
Calling out foolishness gives me such content-
ment

Deal with the root of a problem. Effects will be
outdated
We need mind transformation Behaviour modi-
fication is overrated

Regretting your genuine expression for how you
utterly feel
That's like saying, "Sorry for being real"

Blaze your own trail. Don't be a pathfinder
First rate seer beats a second rate blinder

Intentions and desires make sure to detach
Attachments mixed with worry creates a sorry
batch

It's ok to disagree. No need for confrontation
Uplift. Keep away from easy lamentation

No one needs approval for their self-esteem
Shine your light bright. Sit back and let it beam

Great minds think alike. Positive minds think
greater
If you can't handle this, I guess I'll see you later

For the Wise

Moderation. Implement in everything
Too much of anything? Good for nothing

Silence. Better than useless chatter
Former is better than the latter

Latter being grown. Former being youth
Adults are more jaded. Children sometimes tell
the truth

Once through the door. Twice out the window
Shallow won't cut. Keep it deep and thorough

They say, "Never say never" but it was said twice
Think before we speak. Rashness could be your
worst vice

Grown folks: "Do as I say and not as I do"
Counterproductive. Nothing new

Practice what you preach
Learn for yourself before you bother to teach

Respect is a command
Far from a demand

Faultfinding, "Pot calling kettle black"
Can't call out your own stuff? Self-evaluation
you lack

Envy and jealousy makes no sense

Blowing out someone else's candle doesn't make
yours brighter. You look stupid, ending up dark
and dense

Karma might be your bitch but I treat her nice
Revenge? Dumb and foolish. Digging up 2
graves. Please think twice

What eats up most inside? Holding a grudge
I got faults too. Who am I to judge?

Keep on dreaming. King or Queen. Cop your
crown
What haters don't know can't shoot down

Stay real in a world full of pretension
Play fool to catch wise (not to mention)

Don't play out to be something you are not.
What you attempt to conceal?
Can work against you. Don't believe? Time will
reveal

Everyone wants to be happy and avoid pain
But, there's no rainbow without the rain

Archetype
3 types of peeps
Fakers, takers, creeps

Just playing
I'm saying

Twigs, lilies and the root
Give the first two kinds the boot

Twigs talk so much. Do nothing. So fake
Don't grab them. You'll bust your ass. They easi-
ly break

Lillies
Only blossom when it's nice. Need much correc-
tion

Roots are bonafide
Bumpy or smooth. They'll stay on the ride

To someone we are one of the three. Choosing
your company wisely is a must
6 billion people and counting. Still so hard to
trust

Pretty Ugly

Physical attributes are nice. personality should be more compelling
Be you with ease. Words unspoken are more telling

Outer beauty will fade
Plastic surgery can't even be an aid

Beauty is skin deep. Ugly is to the bones
Wolves among sheep. Masquerading as Al Capones

The fountain of youth we try to maintain
Make up puts natural beauty in disdain

Fake while insides rot
Too stupid to realize beauty can't be bought

Commodifying the soul. Devastating defiance
Fall low to what's in with utter compliance

Don't allow physical things to affirm what's within
The freeing up of our minds need to truly begin

Wondering
Judge based on the energy they exude
Faith in humanity needs to be renewed

Your mind is better than the opinions of others
We feel it deepest when pain and pleasure come
from mothers

Emotions make us feel. Dare not say a word
Screaming inside. Can't be heard

Balanced reciprocity
Alleviates animosity

Constant mutuality
Accentuates sensuality

Lamenting in the past
Will cause regression fast

The presence is a gift
Hold onto good to keep adrift

Future mystery
Mental sores. Blistery

Face alienation
Overcome humiliation

Check your mentality. Question the norm
Embrace your originality. Refuse to conform

Truth

A single lie creates doubt in every truth ex-
pressed
I wanna let my guard down. Put my mental
turmoil at rest

Needs no apology
Dichotomizing mythology

Causes an offense
Runs from pretence

Sets us free
Wouldn't you agree?

Those scared? Look at it with fright
Takes courage to stomach with all one's might

Like rubber, diminishes after each error
We all could use one less stroke. The collapse is a
hoax. Babylon's the terror

Love to hear lies when you know the opposite
Recession is contrived. There is no deficit

Tell the truth. No need to remember anything
Emancipation from deception. Joy it will bring

Beginning of End

Death. Inevitable. No need to mourn
Physical to spiritual. Walking dead we should
scorn

Dying to live. Just living to die
Sounds morbid. "Reality" is a big lie

What's worse than death is what dies inside
Find your passion
Find your drive

Ponder

Forgive yourself. Move on
Clocks ticking. Time forever gone

Secret to failure? Please everyone
Careful of your decisions. Can't be undone

Superhuman? Toughest of people fold
Kindly reminded of this. Lines in concrete show
this bold

Never fear change. Fear stagnation
It's inevitable. Like death and inflation

Put a smile on someone's face. Don't fake your
own
Ku Klux Klan pisses me off too. Have you seen
their upside-down cone?

Better to be hated for who you are than loved for
something you're not. An ugly personality de-
stroys a pretty face
Need more than makeup in this case

Best way to appreciate something? Be without it
for a while
When given a yard. Why not take a mile?

Our deepest cravings can lead to our worst
detriment
What will you choose? Self-destruction or self-
embetterment?

Learn and apply your knowledge
Some educated fools graduate from college

Honesty kills in a world full of make-belief
Causing bad sorrows. Good grief

Everything we hope would last
Ends up inevitably in our past

Giving up can mean you are strong enough to let
go
You want to fly? Give up the things that keep
you low

Crossroads

Avoid love or simply fall?
Say too much or nothing at all?

Be brutally honest or be a crook?
Turn the page or close the book?

Cop an Escalade or a Range Rover?
Fix what's broken or start all over?

Lessons in Friendship

Careful who you open up to. The rest are curious
Very few actually care. Keep the rest oblivious

Taken for granted? Don't be afraid to walk away
Tried your best and nothing happened? Don't be
afraid to go astray

Promises mean everything
Broken? Sorry means nothing

Those who talk behind your back
Prove you are in front of them. Courage to be
real they lack

Real people simply are. Perfect people cease to
exist
Love or leave them with their flaws. Fake ones
shouldn't make the list

Happiness without those you thought you need-
ed most. Nice to realize
Blessing in disguise

Past Lovers

After the first heartbreak, he still wants to be
friends
Had to work through my feelings. It all depends

He found another. Didn't last
Misled me. Believed his lie fast

Fooled myself. Move onto another
Same thing. Different lover

Was insecure. I'll admit
Patience ran short quick. What was the sense to
commit?

Couldn't wait a month. Made that girl your wife
Validates my insecurity. Felt lost in life

Desperate for direction. Hoped this older man
would help my heart mend
Too bad. Wasn't different from my younger
lovers. Would be three times before we finally
came to an end

Three times a charm
What a sorry cliche. Heart endured unnecessary
harm

Thought the fourth was refreshing. Claimed he
was Schizo
Could have been crazy in love. Must have
turned into a ditz though

Found the fifth
Thought he was a gift

If I stayed past that month, I'd be lonesome
By myself, I'll be wholesome

Young and dumb was I? Perhaps
Don't want another. Heart will collapse

Arbitrary

Drunken cowards don't tell tails. Not afraid of
the reaction
Sober heroes don't always speak. Lacking satis-
faction

Get rich or die trying?
Prostitutes purchase getting laid. Deep down?
They're crying

Ganga smoking escapists get a temporary high
Non-smoking realists don't need Mary Jane's
plane to fly

Don't take life too seriously. You'll never get out
alive
Don't wanna fall in love? Learn to dive

Nice to be important. More important to be nice
If stolen, pay double the price

Little Secret

Was wrong. Knew you had a girl
Couldn't resist. Out of this world

Didn't feel guilty. She's not your wife
You claim I drifted away. Just retreating to avoid
potential strife

Homewrecking. Too much to bear
Where do we go from here?

Journey is Destination

Being different makes us the same. See yourself
in others
Giving birth. Commonality amongst mothers

Define by how you grow. Your experiences never
define you
Subtle affirmation of the human experience we
go through

Good to strive
Better to arrive

Don't fear rejection
No such thing as perfection

It's an illusion
Keep afloat. Don't drown in confusion

Like strengths, weaknesses are inevitable
How you deal with life makes you credible

Pride will get rid of you. Humility will keep you
around
What goes up must come down

Keep criticism constructive
Lies told with a smile are destructive

The truth may cause an offence
Progression needs to commence

Better to be peaceful than to be right

Know when to put up a fight

Unwilling to bend?
Relevance is as new as yesterday's fashion trend

Rigid plans gotta go
Gotta go with the flow

Like Nas and Ms. Hill, if I ruled the world, I
would get rid of hunger
Grown folks keep dreaming. You ain't getting
any younger

MLK fought for civil rights
Gandhi. Non-violent. Resisted at peaceful
heights

Castro stood up for Cuba against imperialism
Mother Theresa. Selfless. Cared nothing for ma-
terialism

List. Endless in range
These leaders manifested change

This is my outlook. When I stand
Everliving. Endlessly expand

After all it's said and done, don't forget to laugh
Teach oneself how to learn. Never-ending craft

Untitled

Keep yourself from those undeserving
Value yourself. Keep reserving

Not the load that breaks you. It's how you carry
it
Used to think the reverse. Must admit

Life's a test
Do your best
Keep it moving like the rest

A fighter and a lady locked in one soul
Jaded thoughts tax my inner child. Humour
transcends grey hair. Getting old

In this world, I feel like a stranger
To conformists, being alien is a danger

Dream big. Hope to heavens it comes true
Imagination can expand your current view

Steal big. Hoping you get away
Reality gets hard. Please don't go astray

Artificial? Let it be. Pursue the real
Can see right through the mask. Be true to how
you feel

Ode to Music

Thanks for your song in A minor
If I played it major, it would B just finer
My ears are hungry for sound with my piano in
sight. I C a beautiful diner
If I play and mess up, I'll remember a D is better
than a failing whiner

Note booked

Chords loaded

Arpeggios taking off

Scale soaring

Augmented by cruise control

Falsetto wind

Harmony landed offload at decrescendo until
the note is booked again

The Point
(Inspired by Gwendolyn Brooks, "We Real Cool"
and Antoine Harris', "Jazz Baby Is It In You")

Been fooled
Are ruled

Get tall

Don't grow

Should seek
Build meek

Break pride
Tears dried

Care light
Feel bright

Flow nice
Roll dice

Do him
Dunk rim

Have doubt
Want out

Stylistic

God is the Ultimate Unseen Mystic
Rainbows after storms show God's artistic
More than the physical. Keep it holistic
Fast and pray. Stay puristic
Pious dichotomies hedonistic
Don't wanna be a statistic
I wanna be more selfless and altruistic
All ain't black and white. Stay coloristic
Genocide is far from humanistic
The greedy run the world and are narcissistic
Pessimism is sad. I'm more optimistic
Different point of views. Ever heard of pluralis-
tic?
Illusion of security is capitalistic
Teaching the masses to be socialistic?
The jealous are antagonist
Forget about your rep. What about your charac-
teristic?
Be assertive. Stay deterministic
Repression ain't cool. Grown expressionistic
Don't follow. Be individualistic

Re.Li.Gion

You may want enlightenment like Buddha
You might be a Rasta championing the 12 tribes
of Israel like Judah

You might believe in that old rugged cross
You might high 5 the pillars and make Allah the
boss

You might have had your own Bar or Bat Mitz-
vah
You might speak Sanskrit and call on Krishna

You might believe in something I neglected to
mention
But why do we allow differing beliefs to create
such tension?

When we all grow old, we gon' be jockin' that
pension
Remembering to be ill-minded while love falls
short of long-term retention?

Cut any with any belief and you will ways get
red
Yet, we act like we the best and ignorance con-
tinues to be fed

Naw, I ain't no Atheist because I know there's
something greater than me
I just don't wanna get caught up in debating
what I can't see

So, like a God-given tree
I just wanna be

Void of titles and man-made semantics
We all need love, let's come up with peace tactics

Cosmic Sanctuary

Universe. No walls

Hell. No floor

Heaven. No sealing

Crazy sun blazing mentally
Moaning wind crying gently
Lonesome moon gazing invitingly

Mercury's kitchen real hot

Pluto's sanitation sure to petition

Supernova's stairs real tricky

Jupiter's living room comfy crates

Venus' bedroom. Lovemaking endless

Merged Flows

Atmosphere. Sublimation
Warm. Walls. Condensation
Hot. Passionate precipitation
Tight. Flowing infiltration
Earth. Sip love's runoff from evaporation

Heat. Lava
Sip eruptions. Java

Wind tapped into the funnel. Our peak. Thunderstorm
Rainfall. Trunk expels seed. Fertilize rainbow

Lifeform

Melinated Entities

Seem to half fast our pride during February
Regurgitation. Black figures. Very wary

Knowledge is power implemented through ac-
tion
Jealousy and envy of one another. Our distrac-
tion

Slavery didn't end at emancipation proclamation
We are too color struck for a unified Black nation

Disorganized from conquest and division
Massa's whip caused a slit. Ignorance deepens
this incision

They oppress us because they fear annihilation
I find solace and Garvey's idea of Black repatria-
tion

Some want freedom. We're not on the same page
Some wanna be puppets and continue on stage

Let's see a mind revolution
You're the only detriment to your evolution

Ma

Storm. Rainbow so sweet
Candy had nothing on your affection Best treat

Back home. Hard knock
Keep Christ. Bonafide rock

9 months you carried me
Perseverance. Couldn't see

Tough cookie.
Far from a rookie

Disagreements without a doubt
Pursuing the forgive route

Will it End?
Greeds scent
Tax man sent
Don't have a cent

Western? The West didn't earn anything Always
stealing from the east

Robin Hood? Robbin' isn't just done in the hood,
blue-collar crimes done by the biggest crooks
turned on by profit
Bribery wouldn't lead me to take a hit

Mother Earth sodomized by industrialization's
injection
Without warning nor protection
Infected with pollution and destruction
Could have been prevented with the contracep-
tion of conservation

The cure is minimalism. Cut back on conspicu-
ous consumption

I got money on my mind
Sounds like they're using currency to colonize
my soul and keep you in a bind

While you chasing that cheddar, I'm gonna walk
with consciousness

Tired of the rat race. Wouldn't wanna be last.
Don't care to finish

Fun.To.Mental

Know something ended for something to begin

That which didn't create you can't sustain you

What your subconscious drools over? Universe
will spit back to you

We are a projection from one dimension into an-
other

Realize with your real eyes

Lie to my face and dishonesty will hurt you the
most
Not as bad as the beef between the East and the
West coast

Entertain?
Why not inner train?

What makes us silly?

Not realizing how smart we really are

We focus too much on the effects

Ever question the cause?
You call it justice with crooked laws

No change? No growth
Plea the 5th or take the oath

Slow Down

Heart's thesaurus. Inarticulate words

Argument bruises. Sore us

Kiss my dreams

Hug my memories

Eye candy. Sweet

Taste it in my mind

He's got that love jones for me and for her, her and her

Can't buy my love gets them with jewels and fur

I'd be a fool to love him from a distance

It's a fatal attraction puttin' up a resistance

I slammed on the pedal of my heart. Told love you are going too fast

I fixed my arteries brake pads. Didn't want to crash into infatuation again

The last time I slammed into swag got my vision broken

Glad it's repaired now

Last time I went down that lane, I let his smooth
talk cause me to skid. Spiralled my lotus flower
balm out of control

No longer blind

I saw the nearest exit off the Charmer's fast lane

Don't want to get hydroplaned by his deceit

I'm an Empress

Been playing chess

Have yet to checkmate my King

Hoping that running back's complement touches
me down with a smile

Battling in the game of love. Going for a home
run

His arms to call home

Golf won't club my plans

No more setbacks

Don't wanna lie with the rebound

I get lonely too

Innerstand

I don't overstand. Superior to none
I don't understand. Inferiority isn't fun

I exist to the world. Belong to no one. Least at all
to my own inception
Blowing hot air from a cool mind Mediated by
lukewarm perception

Misery loves company. I'm happy alone
Crying wolf will leave you with an endless
moan

Need I not rush? Time doesn't speed up
Sweet and low spoils my buttercup

I don't know what the future holds but I know it
holds something
Don't give up and do all that for nothing

Concretely Abstract

Dwelling in the past robs the present

Setting up the future

To be duct-taped with nostalgia

Suffocating the breath of imagination

As hope's heartbeat skips

From fear's anxiety

While tying up the feet of freedom

Held hostage by envy

Beating up the embodiment of resilience

As blood comes down the nose of perseverance

Dried by the swift draft of stagnation

Left for death because time is flying

As faith resuscitates hope's flesh

Dare to survive? Fate is preparing its eulogy

No need to mourn

Thank God for transcendence, multiple dimen-
sions

No need to cry

From reality's teasery

He will no longer stick out his tongue

Making fun of your perception

Fear the known. Unknown is reassuring

Everyday
Be merry. Not just on Christmas

Respect the womb that births. Not just on Mother's Day

Respect the seed sower that nurtures where he plants. Not just on Father's Day

Love like we'll never see each other again. Not just Valentine's

Seek a permanent resolution for every problem. Not just New Year's

Be grateful for what good we have. Not just Thanksgiving

Continuously teach ourselves to learn. Not just at school

Celebrate ourselves as an entity who has the gift of life. Not just our birthday

Make an amends before a death day

Take it one day at a time

That's all we get

You Should Know
(Inspired by, "The Alchemist")

Can't give what you don't have

Might be out of my league. It won't stop me
from acknowledging you (you should know)

Sometimes people don't teach you

You simply learn from them

Darkest hour just before dawn (you should
know)

Not loving yourself?

External affirmations useless

Sometimes, relinquishing power? Most powerful
thing to do (you should know)

Too absorbed by the trees?

Might never get out of the forest

Best to be intrinsically priceless than feel like a
million bucks (you should know)

Reeking of righteousness comes from the whiff
of a repent. Adoring the aroma of your descent
(you should know)

Realize what's worth your heart to expend its energy on

Those who gossip to you will eventually gossip about you (you should know)

Wisdom is avoiding all thoughts that weaken you

Those who anger you, control you (you should know)

How you treat and make people feel is all that matters when you're just a memory (you should know)

Superstition is an unnecessary burden to bear

Love is distinct from possession (you should know)

The fear of suffering is worse than suffering itself

Every blessing ignored is a curse (you should know)

We seem to see the world based on what we want instead of what it is

Everyone knows how others should live but none of their own (you should know)

Can't solve a problem if it's trapped inside your mind. It's a discussion blind (you should know)

If you don't care to fight anymore, you have inner peace

My take on things

Just thought

You should know

For Earthlings

Completion signals new start
Don't give into fears. Talk with your heart

Using weakness against others renders you
weakest

Daggers in some smiles, every laugh isn't light-
hearted

Authority is one thing. Control freak is another

Highest form of control? Know when to let go

Nothing is by chance

Everything happens because it has to

No long term decisions on temporary feelings

Emotions can be calmed with the breath

Evolving is like sounding the notes of a scale

As we play on instruments

So the universe on us

Noise shatters silence. Music enhances it

Speech is musical. Quiet is magical

Truth speaks

Denial slows down self-discovery. Tell the truth or say nothing. Less to remember

Empty mind prepared to see the truth

Highest calling? Be true to oneself

Greatest battles? Fought within

Soul must be freed. Whatever the cost

Words hurt. Choked by racists red necks. Broken by the lies of politricks

So silly. GPS couldn't track stupidity

Ignorance off the radar

Pretension's compass

Being overlooked? Sometimes a blessing

No rejuvenation without breakdown and decay

Don't let inspiration run out of ink. Make sure it's held by limitlessness

For every story told, listen to what's not being said

If food is for thought, make sure you're being properly fed

Random thoughts & sage advice in Felicia Guy-Lynch's Scattered Thoughts: A Stream of Consciousness (5/2/13)

Felicia Guy-Lynch's first book, Scattered Thoughts: A Stream of Consciousness, is a poetry collection of random thoughts and shared wisdom on love, self-worth, trust and living in this world. Political, analytical, with word play, rhymes and rhythms – it sometimes feels like you're reading a sheet of music with no notes on it, but you can hear the words, feel the beat.

I saw Guy-Lynch perform "you should know," which appears near the end of Scattered Thoughts, at Glad Day Bookshop back in September at the monthly The Beautiful & the Damned poetry and music cabaret. Having now experienced this piece both live before an audience and read silently to myself in solitude, it's still one of my favourites. Inspired by The Alchemist, the piece imparts sage advice that strikes home and sticks: "…those who gossip to you will eventually gossip about you. you should know wisdom is avoiding all thoughts that weaken you. those who anger you control you. you should know how your treat and make people feel? that's all that matters…"

Often served up with a rap rhythm, some of the poems use rhyme, some don't – and poems like "stylistic" weave a single rhyme throughout the piece. At times, the words flow across the page without punctuation, capital letters signalling the beginning of the next line. And just when you think you've got the rhythm down, anticipating the next beat, Guy-Lynch changes it up, playing the words in rhyming couplets in "crossroads," then floating them in free association phrases in "cosmic sanctuary."

- Cathy McKim
www.lifewithmorecowbell.com